KIVA WATERS

What You Say to Your Self Matters the Most

Any member of educational institutions wishing to photocopy part or all of the work for classroom use, or anthology, should send inquiries to: Kiva V. Waters, c/o Het Hru, POB 230628, Brooklyn, NY 11223.

Created in the United States of America

First softcover edition published: March 2020

FIRST EDITION

ISBN: 978-1-09833-128-3
eISBN: 978-1-09833-129-0

Library of Congress Cataloging-in-Publication data is available for this title.

For good people all over the world,

and for

"Du Rag" girls like

Lala, Lizzy & my Self.

CONTENTS

PROLOGUE

I am a product of the hood.

I was born on Halsey Street in the United States in the 70s, raised on Nostrand Avenue at the intersection of Park Place.

That's Crown Heights aka Crime Heights. Brooklyn, New York to be exact.

It could have been any ruthless environment in New York City, but a wall set us apart from the neighboring communities. Our wall honors dozens of fallen angels from our hood with their names and dates of births and death.

It's a commemorative mural / visually disturbing graveyard. It's fading out nowadays but my best friend's little brother's name is still there. My next door neighbor is there, too. My childhood friends are there. Over thirty people secured an unfortunate spot on that dubious wall before I turned 16. All died way too young.

All fell victim to three of the most lethal summers of my "NA Rock" childhood (read *The Crack Era* by Kevin Chiles) when money, drugs and death were as prolific as the rap guru/cultural icon, B.I.G. aka Biggie Smalls, before he too, was robbed of his bright future in the 90s. Brooklyn.

The wall is a constant reminder to us that Bobby "Blue" Bland was right when he crooned, "Ain't no love in the heart of the city."

My skin grew tough as nails. Early in my life I learned a golden rule: "Trust no one, except God and my mother, of course." My mother was the enforcer and that was one of her two rules. The other: "Get good grades."

I was my mother's first American born child. I was expected to do big things, so I followed those two rules to the tee. I was the District 22 Spelling Bee Champion several years in a row. I was valedictorian of my elementary and junior high schools and I went on to attend Stuyvesant, the top high school in the country still to this day. But life, my life, was far from a "crystal stair." When you enter the work force at fourteen, twenty more years fly by like a 60-second roller coaster ride.

When I was fifteen, my godbrother, Robert, was murdered in front of his home, right around the corner from my home. He was seventeen. Seemed like we were all living fast and dying faster. I bore my first son at eighteen and my second at twenty-three. So, relatively speaking, my childhood was fast, and HARD. I partied hard: Sometimes four nights in a row. I prayed hard: Wednesday nights with Caribbean Baptists AND Sunday mornings with Southern Baptists. These two sects couldn't be more different but I loved them both. I talked hard, too. My voice was so loud I often hurt my own eardrums. Teachers constantly begged me not to scream out answers. The correct answers.

I fought hard. Sometimes two days in a row, but mostly with my words.

I laughed hard. I studied hard. I worked hard. I cried crazy hard. And, I loved super hard.

I enjoyed my childhood as much as possible under the circumstances. My mother was a home attendant and she earned about a hundred dollars a week. Our rent was about three hundred dollars a month. Add it up and it's not difficult to figure out that we often came up short. Short on substantive food. Short on bill-paying money. Short on funds for anything not completely vital to our survival. Young Kiva was well aware of these financial woes because my mother told my siblings and me everything. Her burden was our burden. There were good times. But what comes to mind when I reminisce about my early years is that everything was so incredibly hard, unnecessarily hard. Even fun was hard. Our lives were pure madness.

Academically, I exceeded my mother's expectations by earning degrees ("not cer-ti-ficates" in my Mama's sternest Trinidadian voice) in accounting, literature, law AND fashion marketing. In that order.

More madness.

But I did pass the New York State bar examination the first time I took it and became a licensed New York attorney courtesy of my GREAT alma mater, CUNY School of Law. I was making an honest living.

I proclaimed myself a financial freedom activist.

A more positive euphemism for "bankruptcy lawyer."

Most importantly, I adhered to my mother's rules and won. I was living her dream, The American Dream.

But, I was unbothered, and unaware of who I really was.

All that quality education and I had never heard of meditation. This now seems like an egregious crime. But nothing (truly alive) stays the same.

My metamorphosis began in 2011. That's the year I attended yoga teacher training. I had tried yoga a few times in college and law school, but I wasn't fully immersed. Then I embarked on a 200-hour yoga teacher training course and my life changed. It sounds dramatic (and I am an Aries) but it's true. It's difficult to put into words, but it was almost as if yoga was seeking me.

My blessed instructors at Yoga People yoga studio (sadly now defunct) made me do it. That's not entirely true. Love actually made me do it. Made me want to trust. Made me want to know. Made me want to master the one thing I could not measure with a state exam or a salary cap. Me.

I was already in love with myself. I had great self -esteem.

But…
What is the purpose of the soul inside this body?
Who am I? No, for real for real, who am I?
The voice in my head, is not the real me?

And you're telling me sitting still and breathing is going to reveal the real me?

Meditating made me feel very vulnerable. My root chakras were shot.

It is not easy to disrobe oneself of a reliable armor, like hardness, especially in the midst of the exact same environment you honed it to perfection in. But the toughness had to be taken off. It was of great use to me growing up in the concrete jungle, but I had to let it go. It was time to say goodbye to that (Brooklyn) self-image of "unstoppableness" as Vybz Kartel would say. I eventually let go of the safety blanket. It had protected me for over thirty years but I had to surrender. In savasana. Over and over and over again. For the whole summer of 2012. No junk food. No sugar. No cigarettes. No going to bed after midnight. Yoga and meditation and journaling and learning and sharing and connecting in an intimate Park Slope yoga studio for four to six hours every day.

It was time to know my Self.

Again, I'm a true Aries. God(dess) of War. My sure fire path to winning wars, throughout my life, was reading, KNOWING as much as I could.

Books literally saved my life, many times.

More importantly, I WANTED to know my Self.

My true SELF. There was no book for that. So I let it go. Not my Brooklyn swag. I was kidding about that. I let go of EGO.

There is a difference between the Self we show the world, the Self we show ourselves, and our true SELF.

I craved savasana, also known as shavasana or resting pose or corpse pose.

That minute or two in peaceful semi-meditation, after a great vinyasa class, was more scrumptious than a big slice of Junior's famous cheesecake, a Brooklyn delicacy.

Sean "P. Diddy" Combs once famously made his group of *Making the Band* pledges walk miles from Manhattan to Brooklyn to fetch him a slice of Junior's cheesecake.

I walk there gleefully, often, to my get own slice(s). I LOVE Junior's cheesecake!

I'm going to great lengths to explain that my savasana cravings were serious!

There, in savasana, I slowly began to know me. The real me. My true SELF.

Not "outside Kiva" or that scared, anxiety-ridden, stressed out voice saying… "You know s/he full of shit." "You better not let him/her play you." "Yeah, right." "Yeah, ok." "Whatever."

"Fuck you!" "Fuck ME!" "I'm ready for they ASS!!!"

"You wanna get between my knees, don't ya?"

You get the point.

I meet my true Self in savasana, resting pose, semi-meditation. Every time.

My true SELF is a Kemetic Goddess.

A happy, healthy and wealthy consort of an Arch Angel. My true SELF is perfectly aligned, in tune with all good things, and connected to all good people, and to the One Universal Creator.

We are all One.

Our Oneness is our greatest power.

May the journey to your Self be sweeter, in some part, because of this, my 1st book, **MEDITATION MADNESS**.

The WAY you speak to your SELF matters the most.

CHAPTER 1:
BREATHE

As your desire to know your true Self gains traction, your willingness to explore new things will grow, too.

When you are ready...
Root down.
This just means sit down as low as you can.

In any comfortable position, get centered.
This means be quiet.

Now, rest your eyelids, slowly and gently.
Be still.
That's it.

Stay here.

Inhale (through your nose).
Exhale (through your mouth).

BREATHE

Inhale slowly. (Through your nose).
Now, close your mouth.
Teeth are separate. Jaw relaxed.
Tongue resting gently in your bottom rack of teeth.
Exhale slower. (Through your nose).
Keep going.
When your mind wanders, gently bring yourself back, to

your breath, by thinking…
Inhale. 1 2 3 4 5 6.
Exhale. 1 2 3 4…..

If you stay here,
every day
for as little,
or as long,
as you like,
all the answers you seek will come,
from within
YOU.

Yes. I'll say it again.

You already know the solutions to every one of your "issues."

If you haven't heard this already from The Secret movie, YOU create your own reality – every second of every day and night of your life – because YOU are the BEST THING SINCE WHITE BREAD!!! But that's stuff for my second book… **NO CELEBRITIES ALLOWED.** Coming soon.

Where are we?

Oh! We're listening.

Listening to your breathing is the start of hearing all the answers.

If you're from a hood like my childhood stomping grounds, this whole thing might sound super wack, lame, corny AND unbelievable.

I get it. I am a real Brooklynite, from the real Brooklyn, not the bracking version. You can believe me when I say, meditation is NOT lame. It's not.

Breathing and listening to your breath is connected with, EVERYTHING in your whole life, from start to finish, soup to nuts, nut to butt, however you like it. This is meditation and it leads you directly to you. To your true true Self. Meditation is the dirtiest, oldest, livest "A" train ride to the one true YOU.

Just BREATHE. No need for any certain mat, although a yoga mat or pillow may help. I like Gaiam mats, bamboo floors and zafus. They feel right for ME. I have expensive habits. I'm from Brooklyn, what more can I say? But NONE of that is required for meditating your way to your true Self.

No need for a water bottle or waist beads or special workout clothes, although quality "dry-fit" apparel can be beneficial, too. Keeps you fresh by wicking away sweat (for us hot folk that get a little damp while meditating).

Just listen to your Self.

Listen to your own breath.

You listen to other people all day. Your voice is most important. Listen.

One inhale at a time.

One exhale at a time.

When you are ready, close your eyes.

Seems simple, and it is.

Still waters run deep.

Meditation is simple and very deep.

Meditating starts REVERSING the EFFECTS of STRESS the very first time you do it. Meditation is a lifelong gift.

DO NOT DWELL IN THE PAST, DO NOT DREAM
OF THE FUTURE, CONCENTRATE THE MIND
ON THE PRESENT MOMENT.   BUDDHA

Meditation also REVERSES decades of MISTRUST.

Mistrust is the ultimate weapon of concrete jungle warriors, like myself. It's a reliable shield, and sword, made for extremely dire situations. And then there's stress, the world's best assassin ever.

Bad news is, stress is more fatal than "The Professional."

Good news is, it can be OVERcome.

> WHEN MEDITATION IS MASTERED, THE MIND
> IS UNWAVERING LIKE THE FLAME OF A CANDLE
> IN A WINDLESS PLANE.   BHAGAVAD GITA.

BREATHE. Still want to know who you really are? Good.

> YOU HAVE A TREASURE WITHIN IN YOU THAT
> IS INFINITELY GREATER THAN ANYTHING THE
> WORLD CAN OFFER.   ECKHART TOLLE

So you must sit still, before all of your other morning routines.

Be still.

> MEDITATION IS NOT EVASION; IT IS A SERENE
> ENCOUNTER WITH REALITY.   THICH
> NHAT HANH

Just be.

Before your tea, coffee, latte, lemon water. Before you wake up the kids.

Before you check Facebook, Twitter and InstaGram. Before YOGA.

Just listen…to your Self…and breathe…for thirty seconds at a time.

Then one minute at a time. Then two minutes. Then three. Six. Nine.

Then COMMIT to nine minutes every day. You got this. Keep going.

BREATHE

To strengthen your meditations, touch your pointer fingers to your thumbs, or rest both palms on your knees, or place palms face up on your thighs.

Try meditating between 4am and 6am to connect to power hours (more on that later).

Then, when you hear and trust your Self, meaning you can differentiate your soul talking to you versus your other voice(s),

AND you are listening to your true Self, first, every day, for about eighteen to thirty days,

AND

you feel a lot less affected by day to day issues as they arise, or

for no reason at all, move on to Chapter 2.

CHAPTER 2:
SALUTE

For good reasons, our ancient ancestors constantly honored the Sun in ritual. We can understand why because it still provides sustenance for us today, hundreds of millions of years later.

SALUTE

We've learned that sunlight, specifically the sun's ultraviolet B rays (UVB), provides the essential Vitamin D that ALL our BODIES NEED to THRIVE.

The more we soak up the Sun, the better we feel. It's a fact. And I'm sure its part of the reason vacations are federally mandated necessary expenses.

The Egyptian Sun God was called Atum. He is a representation of creation. That big, bright yellow ball that rises in the east and sets in the west is a massive creative power source, which is where we get the term power hour.

Power hour is a sacred time, when universal energy is at its strongest. Anytime between 4am and 6am falls within the power hour time range because the sun exerts the most metaphysical strength right before it rises.

Your power hour can also be the time you wake up to begin your day, even if that happens in the evening because your work may not be 9 to 5.

Your personal power hour can also be around sunrise, sunset or ANYTIME.

No matter what path you are on, if you want to know your true Self, you must first salute (greet) the new day during YOUR power hour.

Every day is best.

A morning salutation honors all beginnings and is the most creative and powerful way to start every new day. I like to call my power hour my "gratitude time" because simply saying thank you, three times in succession in a hale and hearty tone, suffices as a proper morning salutation. Then I can get on with my day in positive ways. That happens sometimes if I've had a long night, hanging out with my HUGE family, and I "don't have time" for my regular 4am to 6am power hour salute.

I still reap all the benefits of my morning salutation just by saying:

"THANK YOU! THANK YOU! THANK YOU!"

while facing the skies and the rising Sun.

Gratitude, for breath, our body temples, for water, food, clothing and shelter, is especially powerful right after meditation.

So as you wake, rise. Just like our late, great Queen Goddess Maya Angelou.

We rise.

Rise up.

Face east.

Don't fret if you don't know which direction is east.

You can (and you will) figure it out on Google later.

For now...

Inhale deeply and raise your arms all the way up.

Your open palms should face the sky.

Hold a breath.

Gaze up.

SALUTE

Then exhale deeply.

Bring your hands to prayer at the center of your chest.

Bring your gaze down and relax your eyelids, jaw and shoulders.

Inhale.

Bring to mind your biggest dreams.

Visualize your will being done.

Exhale.

Let go of lingering stress, doubt, and worry.

Blow obstacles away literally with your breath.

Then inhale.

Open your eyes.

Stretch your arms back up to the sky.

Hold.

Exhale. Fold in half at the waist.

Forget about touching your toes for now.

Hang loose.

Don't bounce.

SALUTE

Ground down through your heels.

Then spread your toes for balance.

Inhale.

Rise up halfway to a flat back.

Palms resting on your shins.

Exhale.

Fold in half again.

Nod your head yes. Gently.

Shake your head no. Gentler.

Now deep inhale.

All the way up to standing position. Slowly.

All the way up. Palms to the sky.

Then deep exhale.

Hands to prayer center.

Eyes soften then close.

That's it.

You have officially saluted the Sun, a true super power.

WISDOM COMES WITH THE ABILITY TO BE
STILL. JUST LOOK AND LISTEN. NO MORE IS
NEEDED.   ECKHART TOLLE

Add this sweetness to your daily meditation.

This is sometimes called a practice. Let your "practice" speak to you, in your own way, to your Self.

There is a voice that does NOT use any words.

Listen to that voice. REALLY. JUST LISTEN.

Trust what you hear.

Then move forward to Chapter 3.

CHAPTER 3:
CREATE

As you meditate and salute the sun every day you will notice you have a lot more energy now to go along with that extra understanding of your Self. Energy yields power. Your power is your health.

HEALTH IS BETTER THAN WEALTH.
DAMIAN "JR. GONG" MARLEY

Your very breath is your power.

Your words are powerful, too.

And yes, money, power, and respect are interrelated just like Lil Kim said. Brooklyn. But taking POSITIVE action, using your powers for good, and for all, is how we receive what we want. We desire happiness, health, and wealth, in different forms. It all takes patience, as my eldest son Sekou would say. And action.

"Just do it" is more than just a Nike slogan. It is a mantra, a mantra for action. In Nike's case, the action they want you to take is to buy their goods. In your case, it's the good actions you take now to fulfill your dreams.

C

R

E

A

T

E

I used to only produce what I thought was my best work, when my back was against a proverbial wall. That was not positive action. That was a re-acting. This was, of course, before I was introduced to my true Self.

EVERYTHING THAT HAPPENS TO YOU IS A REFLECTION OF WHAT YOU BELIEVE ABOUT YOUR SELF.   QUEEN GODDESS DR. IYANLA VANZANT

Then I read *Sacred Woman* by Queen Afua, bestselling author, Spiritual Teacher, Holistic Health Practitioner and Mother of Womb Wellness. Brooklyn. Now, I have the inside right, so the outside just falls into place.

I am still first. When I move, I am perfectly in tune with universal timing. Usually.

But my abundance is ALWAYS acquired (and multiplied just like the Bible says) through sharing.

I give because I TRUST ENERGY and the circular nature of positive money vibes. This means all that I share, returns to me over and over again, tenfold.

> ANONYMOUS TO ANONYMOUS. WE GON' TAKE
> IT THERE. I PROMISE THIS.   SEAN CARTER

Anonymous to anonymous sharing being the ultimate means to unlimited happiness, health, and wealth. It means giver does not know to whom they are giving, and receiver doesn't know from whom they are receiving.

Sharing, for me, is about, "Whom did I treat well today?"

That's the question on my mind at the end of every day.

One of my personal goals is to become a billionaire by positively impacting billions of people and empowering good people all over the world to unite, and invest in love.

That's a major key.

Love is the most majorest key.

Love is the key that opens all doors.

Gratitude swallows all fears.

So go ahead.

Do something.

Anything loving.

You can think of something you want right now, right?
Go ahead.

Do something random and loving to help someone
in need.

Don't overthink it. Go with your first thought.

C

R

E

A

T

E

What you want, in fact, EVERYTHING you want, will move closer
and closer to you, not only as you think about, and plan for it,
but as you serve others, sincerely, while waiting for "it" to arrive.

The first time (and every time) you step out on faith and lend someone a helping hand, share a knowing grin, hug a domestic animal or a tree, or invest a couple hundred dollars in a good friend's start up idea, or hold a door open as a 90 year old lady and her walker slowly gets through it, you open universal portals to your biggest dreams. Every loving deed you can think of creates a fundamental energetic conspiracy to get you whatever it is YOU want. You become an abundance accumulator, a magnetic force drawing in the objects of your desire bit by bit.

Don't do anything rash. Hasty and impulsive moves tend to take people out of their true characters.

Small, genuinely loving gestures set strong positive energies in real motion.

Like helping a digitally challenged person complete a computer task or making someone a vegetable omelet or paying a visit to a senior living facility or giving a complete stranger a compliment. Go ahead. Try it.

Take action. Make positive change.

Whatever you do— no matter what it is—will create a ripple, like a pebble dropped in a pond.

CREATE

Waves go out.

Waves come in.

That is energy.

You don't have to know what $E = mc2$ means to know that you can trust energy.

When you know your Self, you begin to master your energy waves. You consciously send out more positive ripples with your good intentions. Your energy, your service to others, can and will, bring you unlimited abundance. Send out shock waves around your local community.

Keep your actions sincere. Be humble.

Sit. Trust.

Rise. Salute.

Then act.

Once you've proven to your Self (the only one that matters) that acting in service of other others is directly related to getting everything YOUR sweet, little heart desires, go forward, on to Chapter 4.

CHAPTER 4:
LISTEN

By now you know that listening is important.

Chapter 1 was all about listening to your Self.

Now that you've been meditating at least nine minutes every morning, and you know your own voice, you can begin to listen to others.

I mean really listen, without judgment. Listen without thinking about what you're going to say next while someone else is talking, and without your thoughts drifting off to your own, more pressing problems.

Just listen.

Listen with your ears AND your eyes and your mind AND your heart and your SOUL.

Simple? No.

Necessary? Yes.

This is the next, crucial step to knowing who you really are:
Listening.

Specifically, listening to communicate. Know that SILENCE can be supportive and powerful, too. Silence is usually the best answer because listening is a form of participation, too.

Learn to be silent while communicating.

> Silence is an art. Practice it AFTER meditation, salute and positive action.

> Communicate with your **Inner G.**

> Your E-ner-gy.

> Share what you learn only with people that tell you they want to know.

Seshat is the ancient Egyptian God/dess of words and knowledge. She is also called *Mistress of the House of Books* and is credited with inventing writing. As you learn to be a silent communicator, think of Goddess Seshat.

LISTEN

Her name means "she who is the scribe," but Goddess Seshat assisted Pharaohs in the "stretching the cord" ritual, a ritual related to laying out the foundations of temples.

She guaranteed sacred alignments and was essential after annual floods to re-establish vital boundary lines.

I believe that Goddess Seshat possessed a supreme LISTENING ability.

She was also the Goddess of Astronomy, Surveying and Architecture.

"The Boss" as Diana Ross would say.

The epitome of a silent, energetic communicator and a powerful listener.

Even thinking of the Goddess Seshat daily, as you desperately try to focus and listen to what someone else is saying, is like trying not to blink when you're dropping Visine in your red, tired eyes. Not easy.

At first.

LISTEN

As you learn more and more about your Self, you will begin to rest your mouth more easily and allow what you see, hear and feel to take precedence in conversations. Expressing your Self in positive energetic ways takes patience.

IT ALL TAKES PATIENCE.   AMERIKOU

Some of us, after years of meditation, still rather talk to communicate. Like me. AGAIN, I'm an Aries, overly dramatic, passionate, love and seriousness, caught up in a bubble of endless babbling (sometimes).

So, I check my words, in advance of speaking them. You can too.

Are they…

1. truthful?

2. necessary?

3. timely?

4. kind?

Here's the kicker: if you answered 'no' to any of the above, be quiet.

L

I

S

T

E

N

Whenever, you find your Self in a position where you are about to say something to another human being, an animal, a plant, a living, breathing thing, or to your Self, that is not true, necessary, timely or kind, just stay still.

Do not talk. Trust me.

Listen. Then, listen some more. Seriously, this takes time.

More intense listening is mandatory to gain more leverage in almost every situation, especially the really tough ones. Believe me, I know.

I'm a 70s baby from Brooklyn remember?

Stay focused like the Goddess Seshat.

Be patient.

Breathe.

Consider re-reading Chapter 1 (and Chapter 2 and Chapter 3) if you always need words.

When you can communicate with energy, at least sometimes, move forward to Chapter 5. Avid Inner-G users, let's go! NOW! It's madness remember?

CHAPTER 5:
RELAX

The "Rat Race" Bob Marley sang about is real. The grind, the hustle, we are all stuck in "go mode" from time to time.

Sometimes it's good. But when it's constant and stifling, it's unhealthy. NYC is go mode times fifty. The U.S. in general is go mode times a hundred.

I can only imagine that Ghana and Vietnam are go mode times a thousand based on their current, rapid economic development.

Taking a break and slowing down will not cause you to lose your destiny or your place in life or your fortune. But, it feels like it sometimes.

In my hood we race to that red light. Then we blow our horns exactly zero point three seconds after that light turns green.

Stressful. The truth is relaxing does not delay anyone's mission.

Relaxing and reflecting actually advances all of our causes. Check out the "work" being done at The Nap Ministry if you think I'm kidding.

Then take a super deep BREATH and relax. Right now.

RELAX.

We receive universal memos, and recharge our positive Inner G, by relaxing.

Restore your Self every single day no matter how long it takes.

We recharge our cell phones every day, religiously.

And that thousand dollar non-living thing still only stays "alive" (unplugged) for about a half a day, at best.

Don't neglect your Self. You are made of cells that work all day, everyday. Brooklyn (Nets) style. Honor your Self.

RELAX

Goddess pose, also known as Supta Baddha Konasona, is my fav yoga pose EVER!!!!!!!!!

You can say it if you RELAX, and go slow. It sounds exactly like it's spelled. I call it "BADDA!" for short and all you really need to know is that it is the epitome of relaxation.

> Exhale and lower your back to the floor, first leaning on your hands. Once you are leaning back on your fore-arms, use your hands to spread the back of your pelvis and release your lower back and upper butt through your tailbone.

Bring your torso all the way to the floor, supporting your head and neck on a soft blanket if needed.

Use your hands to grip your topmost thighs and rotate your inner thighs externally, pressing your outer thighs away from the sides of your torso.

Slide your hands along your outer thighs, from hips to knees, and widen your outer knees away from your hips.

Now slide your hands down along your inner thighs, from knees to groins.
Stay.

Imagine that your inner groin is sinking into your pelvis.

Push your hip points together, so that while the back pelvis widens, the front pelvis narrows.

Lay your arms on the floor, angled at about 45 degrees from the sides of your torso.
Palms up.

The natural tendency in this pose is to push the knees toward the floor in the belief that this will increase the stretch.

But pushing the knees down will harden your groin, belly and lower back.

Instead, imagine that your knees are floating up toward the ceiling and continue settling your groins deep into your pelvis.

As your groins drop toward the floor, so will your knees. Stay here like this. RELAX.

The first time you do it you might only want to be here for a minute. You will gradually extend your stay. Once, you fall in love with the feeling of bliss that comes over you as your knees descend further and further towards the ground beneath you, you won't be able to resist.

Stay here as long as you want. For now.

Anywhere from five to ten minutes is like giving your Self a full body massage.

No cap. RELAX.

To come out of Goddess pose, use your hands to press your thighs together, then roll over onto one side and push yourself away from the floor, head trailing the torso.

Physical intimacy with someone you love helps our bodies to relax, too. And red wine.

And dark chocolate.

But Supta Baddha Konasana did it for me when I was caught in the rat race for longer than normal and got my Self hurt, real bad.

Goddess pose will forever be my "go-to" asana from there on out. Intuit which you prefer. Then, take a day off. No work. No play. No spouse, kids or family. No friends. Just you.

Solitude is the best way to relax as you become more aware your Self.

Solitude means being alone.

You are a solo act.

Even if you are married with a shoe full of children like "Mother Goose," there is just YOU at the beginning and end of every day.

Being alone is a very important form of self-care. It is a time to be treasured.

This is great news.

ONE IS THE MAGIC NUMBER.   JILL SCOTT

One really is a magical number. (And three, six, seven and nine, too.)

So relax.

Relaaax.   RELAX

Remember your mission.

Who are you meeting for the first time?

Your Self.

Your mental, physical and spiritual Self needs relaxation to fully recharge.

Your mind, body and soul do not function properly, individually or as a team as they should, without GOOD rest. FYI: three hours is not good rest.

The time you reserve for your SELF will enhance the time you spend with ALL of your loved ones, friends, clients and even complete strangers.

One more chapter to go...

Be still.

Slow it down a bit.

CHAPTER 6:

BE YOUR SELF

You will get used to LIVING and moving around with positive vibes, 24/7, **365.**

It will become second nature to be happy all the time, to choose love first when problems arise, to trust and to be kind and compassionate all the time.

And to just be, like the fish in the oceans.

They are not flailing and gasping for air. Fish are, generally, at peace.

Peace is the ultimate mission of meditation.

Some say enlightenment. Others use the word bliss to describe it. I say, I am at peace.

Happy people are at peace.

Healthy people are at peace.

Wealthy people are at peace.

Knowledge of Self brings us all into a mutually harmonious state of being.

Peace is an infinite space.

So is our potential.

BE YOUR SELF.

And just like that. You are limitless.

MAGIC(K).
Stardust, literally.

Unbounded, unrestrained,
unfathomable Oneness with the
entire multiverse.

YOU.

Welcome to your Self …
Namaste.

(This means the star "light" within me, honors the star "light" within you.)

And remember, the way you speak to your Self matters the most.

EPILOGUE

It must be noted here that meditation is NOT a panacea or a quasi-religious, neo-philosophical, cure all. Meditation will not cure cancer (Dr. Sebi already did that) or magically wipe away all of our daily problems.

That being said, if you are alive, you are still in the game, so to speak.

You are still riding the wave of life and your heartbeat proves it. You wavy!

The ups and downs of life are non-negotiable.

The way you speak to your Self matters the most.

HEY, WHAT HAVE I GOT? WHY AM I ALIVE ANYWAY? NINA SIMONE

YOUR EVERY BREATH IS A MIRACLE.

Meditation is your tool, your ticket to getting this life "right" based on guidance from your all-knowing (absolutely Divine) Self.

To get the most from this tool, this **MEDITATION MADNESS**, think of it as more hammer than book. Use it regularly to hammer your way through life and keep introducing yourself to the newest, best, most complete version of YOU.

There are no pictures in this tool-book.

Here, readers get carte blanche to create a meditation practice based on what feels good, rather than what they see.

Meditation is not a cure-all but it is has been scientifically proven to reduce loneliness, anxiety, inflammation, chronic pain, depression, the symptoms of irritable bowel syndrome, blood pressure and heart disease.

That's with NO "side effects."

Meditation also improves sleep, immune systems, empathy, attention, focus, test scores and stress management.

Dr. Elizabeth Hoge, a psychiatrist at the Center for Anxiety and Traumatic Stress Disorders at Massachusetts General Hospital and an assistant professor of psychiatry at Harvard Medical School, told Harvard Health Letter, "...You might think 'I'm late, I might lose my job if I don't get there on time, and it will be a disaster!'

Mindfulness teaches you to recognize, 'Oh, there's that thought again. I've been here before. But it's just that — a thought, and not a part of my core self.'"

Just breathe.

That is meditation.

ACKNOWLEDGMENTS

The highest thanks to the Most HIGH GOD, and all the Goddesses and Gods. A ginormous thanks to Wendy Chanelis for graciously offering me the chance to grow. Thanks to Fern Langham, Kevin Bachman, Abel Costa, Donnalynn Civello, Katelin Sisson, Julia Haramis, Queen Afua, Dr. Iyanla Vanzant, Urban Asanas Owner, Jyll Hubbard-Salk, to the earth, Nostrand Av, Brooklyn, Stuyvesant HS, Temple University, and NYU, to the fire, CUNY Law School, the Brooklyn Bar Association, and LIM College and to my air, Crunch Flatbush. An ETERNAL THANK YOU to ALL my Waters, James, Brown, Clemonts, Donaldson, St. Louis, Pollidore, Mensah, Park Pl, ATL, Maryland, Trinidad& Tobago family. **All of your beautiful souls, and all the stories we share, inspire me to write.**

To my mother, Gloria aka Sugah Plum, I dedicate this book to you, my first example of strength, perseverance and soulful beauty. To my loving husband, my support, my Michael, you are the best man in the whole world, irreplaceable. To my kings, my sons, my phenomenal bonus daughters, you ALL are my life, literally. To my inspirational mother in law, my "Naomi" and all my sisters and brothers, I love you all forever. To all my nieces, nephews, cousins, aunts, uncles and my soul sisters, Shana, Mia, Helen, Rosie and Tyesha, the world is mine, yours and OURS. To my wise beyond her years book editor, Tracee Loran, Owner of The Socialite Design, you already know. And to my heart that beats outside my body, my UNBELIEVABLY CUTE, PERSONALITY-FILLED and LIMITLESS granddaughters, Alani Seliné aka Lala, and Aleise Glory aka Lizzy, your sweet voices matter the most to me.

A Welcome from the Dean

On behalf of all who work and worship here, I welcome you to Chichester Cathedral. I hope this book will help you to enjoy your visit, and will provide a continuing source of interest and reflection when you have returned home.

Chichester Cathedral has its origins in the 11th century and contains examples of the finest architecture and art from that century to our own, not least a collection of 20th-century religious art.

The main purpose of the cathedral is the worship and praise of Almighty God, and we are pleased to welcome visitors to our services, of which Choral Evensong, on most days during school terms, is enduringly popular.

I hope you will have time to spend some moments in prayer or reflection during your visit. If so, perhaps you would remember all who minister here, and who have the privilege and responsibility of maintaining the fabric and the life of this great church.

If you would like to visit our refectory in the Bell Rooms, it is situated in the cloisters, and offers a range of refreshments to visitors from Monday to Saturday.

Nicholas Frayling

The history of the cathedral began not at Chichester but at Selsey, ten miles to the south. There, in AD681, Saint Wilfrid, formerly Abbot of Ripon and Bishop of York, came as an exile from the North, and was granted land by King Aethelwealh to build a cathedral. Shortly afterwards Caedwalla of Wessex conquered the little kingdom, but he confirmed the grant to Wilfrid and himself became a Christian.

The Normans, however, in accordance with their general policy, removed the see in 1075 to Chichester, the former Roman town of *Noviomagus*, where there already was a church dedicated to St Peter (subsequently incorporated in the cathedral).

The site was central, and Chichester Cathedral has, therefore, from its beginning related intimately to the city and its community. Construction began under Bishop Stigand in about 1076, and was vigorously continued by Bishop Ralph de Luffa (1091–1123). Although a fire in 1114 hindered progress, much of the building as we know it existed by 1123 – the nave, the transepts (with eastern chapels), the quire and three eastern chapels, the centre one being a short Lady Chapel. All the chapels had apsidal (rounded) ends. The essentially Romanesque character of the cathedral is what Luffa made it, its prototype being the *Abbaye aux Hommes* at Caen.

ABOVE RIGHT: *St Wilfrid established the Church in Sussex in the late 7th century.* ㉑

ABOVE: *An artist's impression of Bishop Luffa's Norman cathedral.*

RIGHT: *The nave, with the Bell-Arundel screen and the Piper tapestry beyond.*

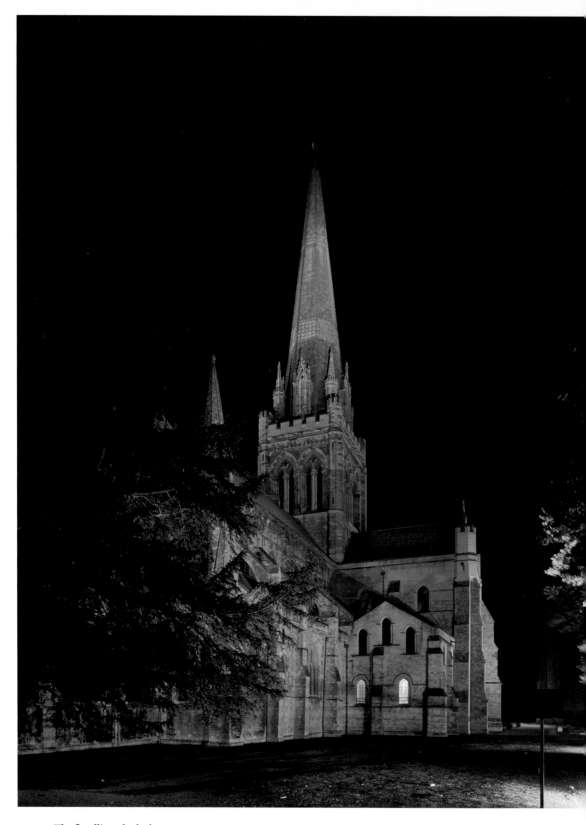

ABOVE: *The floodlit cathedral.*

In the last decades of the 12th century there was an important development under Bishop Seffrid II (1180–1204), formerly Dean. In 1187 a second great fire burned the wooden roof and damaged extensively the east end of the building. So stone quadripartite vaulting and a new clerestory were introduced. The somewhat severe Norman arches were flanked by pointed arches. Purbeck marble shafts were added, as were slender stone shafts from floor to roof, and flying buttresses strengthened the structure.

But the most impressive achievement of this new work was the two-bay retroquire, designed in the Transitional style, yet in its proportions harmonizing with the rest of the building.

ABOVE: *The restored south-west tower.* ①

The arch of the arcade is rounded; the gallery has two pointed arches under a round one, and at the east end are complex sculpture and decoration. But the most elegant features of this sophisticated advance on Luffa's building are the big central Purbeck shafts in the retroquire which are surrounded by four others, free-standing and of the same stone, with delicate foliage capitals. As part of this development the side chapels were squared off, and the Lady Chapel (also squared) was extended, forming the first two bays of the present chapel.

In this way Seffrid enriched what Luffa had done, and provided what today is regarded, indeed is visibly evident, as the architectural climax of the cathedral. This was shown when Seffrid rededicated the cathedral in 1199 in honour of the Holy Trinity. Trinity Sunday was decided upon as the appropriate day for offerings to be made from the whole diocese.

ABOVE: *The Gothic south quire aisle.* ⑩

In the 13th century there were further additions. The two chapels in the transepts achieved their present shape (St Pantaleon in the south with its elegant capitals, and the Chapel of the Four Virgins in the north). Five nave chapels were also added: St Clement and St George to the south and St Thomas (Becket), St Anne and St Theobald to the north. The southern chapels remain, but on the north side St Thomas alone still exists (dedicated also to St Edmund of Abingdon, and restored and refurbished in recent times).

The Early English style is also characteristic of the three main porches, of which the first was St Richard's, now the entrance from the western arm of the cloister. Each porch has a vaulted roof and an entrance sub-divided into two bays with a central column, and each has varied ornamentation. The north porch is less impressive than St Richard's, and the west porch (where modern glass doors have been inserted) has been extensively remade.

The present Canons' Vestry, off the south transept, was built after St Richard's Porch, an addition to the Early English work, with five-part vaulting and elaborate foliage ornament and bosses.

The period 1245 to 1253, despite its brevity, was very important in the cathedral's history because of the episcopate of Richard of Wych (St Richard of Chichester), following which the cathedral became a great centre of pilgrimage. The vindication of Richard's cause against King Henry III (who at first was hostile to his election as bishop), his sanctity, his pastoral zeal, and, finally, his canonization in 1262, inspired great devotion. The Saint's body, which had lain near the Chapel of St Thomas and St Edmund (the latter his friend and mentor), was moved on 16 June 1276 in the presence of King Edward I to a platform situated in the retroquire.

Pilgrims came in great numbers to his shrine. It was destroyed in the reign of Henry VIII, but in recent years the site (where an altar now stands) has regained its significance as a holy place for thousands of modern pilgrims. What is believed to be a bone of St Richard was interred beneath the altar in 1992. The Prayer of St Richard is a familiar and greatly loved expression of Christian aspiration and discipleship. The Anglo-German tapestry forms a focus for devotion.

LEFT: *A statue of St Richard near his shrine.* ⑫

RIGHT: *Holy Communion in the Chapel of St Thomas and St Edmund.* ⑳

INSET RIGHT: *A corbel from the library depicting toothache.* ⑰

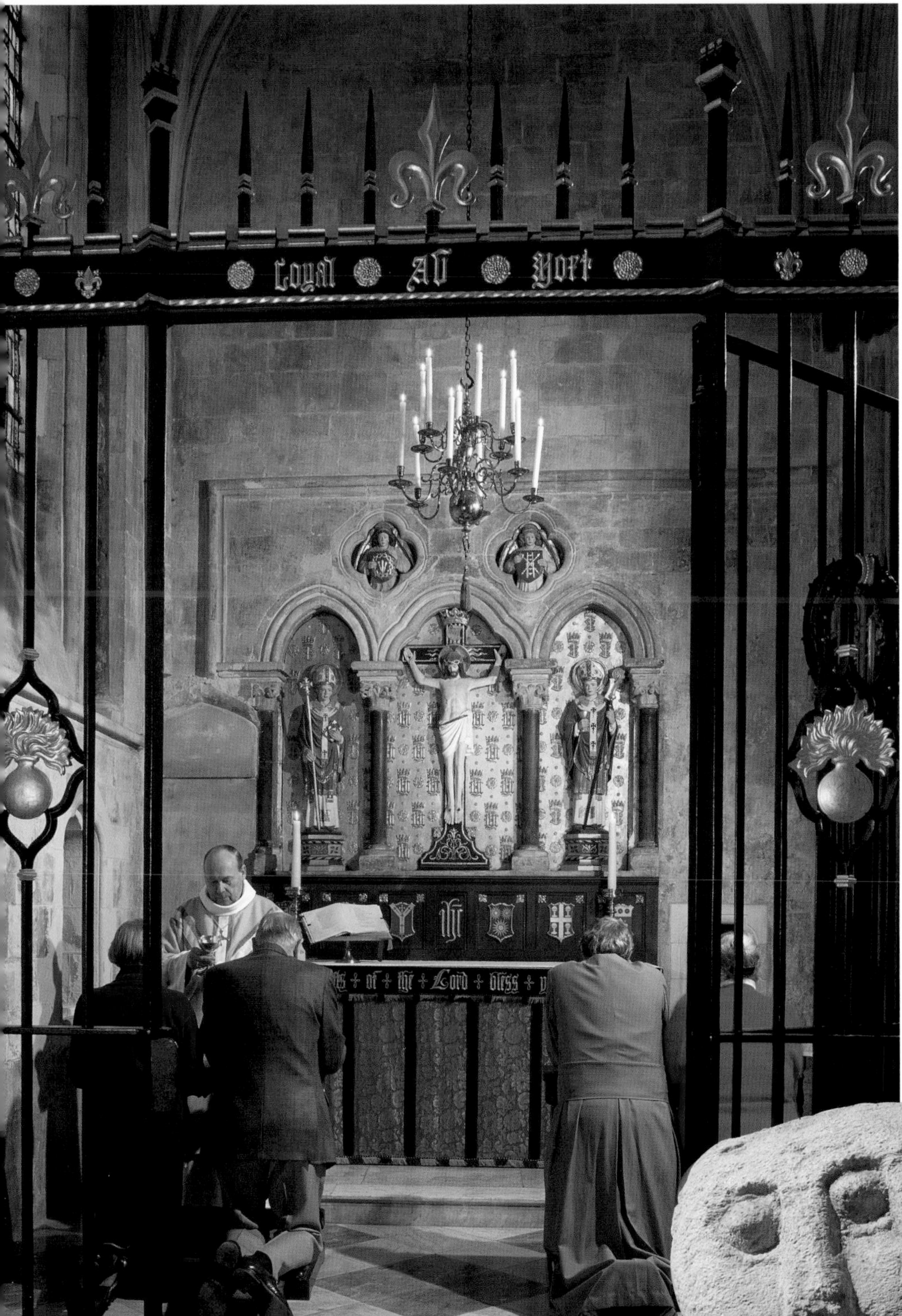

THE 13TH CENTURY

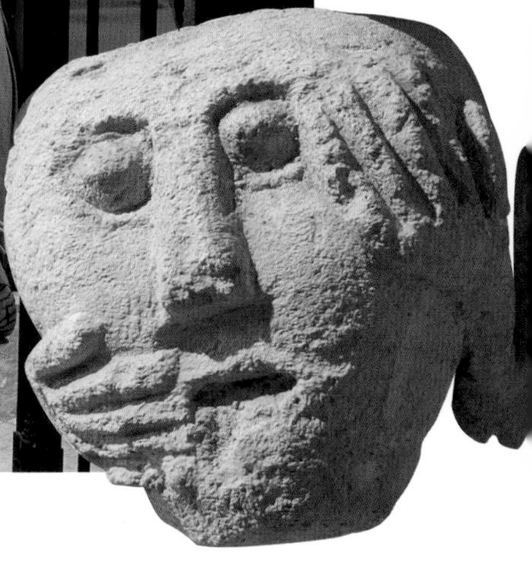

ABOVE: *The choir at weekday choral evensong.* ⑦

In the last years of the 13th century the extension of the Lady Chapel to its present length was completed and its windows, as they now are, were inserted. The glass is modern.

John Langton, who became Bishop in 1305 and was Chancellor of England, was responsible for a major change in the appearance of the south transept when he introduced the immense window. It has been suggested that the tomb beneath the window is Langton's, but the effigy does not fit the embrasure, and there is no other evidence to substantiate the claim.

The 14th century gave us the quire much as it now is. The stalls date from about 1330: their canopies and detached shafts and ogee arches are original, though the panelling is Victorian. They were restored after the fall of the spire in 1861, and the stalls of the Dean and Precentor at the western end are of that later period. The misericords, hinged seats which enabled elderly and infirm priests to lean while standing (*misericordia*

ABOVE: A misericord of a fox playing a harp, with a goose and a dancing ape. ⑦

means pity or compassion), are of the same period as the original stalls. The design of the carvings, fortunately little damaged when the spire fell, has no overtly religious significance. Some of them incline to the grotesque, and the number of such supporting heads in reverse makes the Chichester set of distinctive interest.

Behind the stalls in the south transept is a stone screen a little later than the stalls themselves, pleasantly and variedly ornamented, with three bays. Erected by Bishop Stratford (1337–62), it contains what is reputed to be his tomb. The effigy, with a dog at his feet, is contemporary, but the tomb chest is modern.

BELOW: The Lady Chapel (c. 1300). The statue Virgin and Child *(1988) is by John Skelton.* ⑭

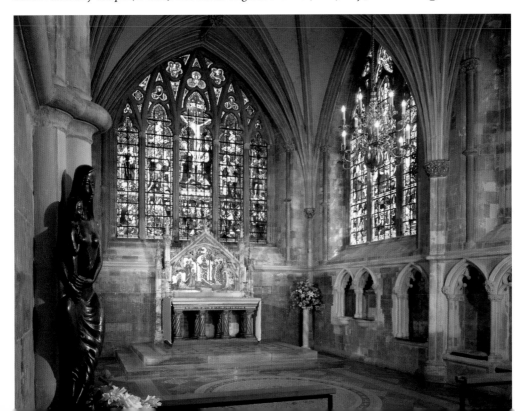

Some features which we now think of as characteristic of Chichester we owe to the 15th century. The cloisters were built about 1400, and the seven-light window in the north transept, early Perpendicular in style, was inserted about the same time, or maybe a little earlier. The Chapter House was also erected over what is now the Canons' Vestry.

In the same period the bell tower was finished. Although several medieval cathedrals once had similarly detached towers, Chichester is the only one to possess a surviving original. It was built to receive the great bells (of which there are now eight) from the central tower. It is not an elegant structure, yet in scale it accords with the main building. It was in this century, too, that the spire – now the most prominent feature – was added. The Arundel screen (named after Bishop John Arundel, 1459–78, but probably early 15th century) immediately strikes the eye as the visitor enters the west door of the cathedral. Originally it shut off the quire, and there were chapels in the two outer arches. The screen was taken down in 1859 (which probably precipitated

ABOVE: The western cloister looking towards St Richard's Porch. The vault is Early English. ④

the collapse of the spire in 1861). It was restored to its original place in 1961 as a memorial to George Bell (Bishop 1929–58). The lierne vaulting and the detail of the sculpture merit close inspection, though the primary importance of the screen lies in its spatial relationship to the whole building.

In 1478 Edward Story was consecrated Bishop of Chichester. The alabaster effigy on the north side of the sanctuary (the canopy is modern) is his memorial. Story was responsible for building the city cross, and he generously endowed the Prebendal School, in West Street, where the cathedral choristers are educated.

LEFT: The 15th-century Bell-Arundel screen, dismantled in 1859 and re-erected in 1961 as a memorial to George Bell, (Bishop 1929–58) pictured below. ⑥

ABOVE: *The bell tower, built c.1400, was once surrounded by houses.* ㉕

Robert Sherburne became Bishop in 1508 and died in 1536. His effigy is in a recess in the south aisle of the quire. Sherburne was a political bishop, secretary to Henry VII, ambassador and royal counsellor. He had also been Dean of St Paul's. He 'steered a prudent course' at the Reformation, and accommodated himself to the changes. He was what is known as an 'Henrician', that is, he accepted the political changes of the King, but was no innovator in doctrine. Determined, like Story before him, to reform the lax ways of the clergy, he endowed four prebends, secured a house for them and appointed a dean, William Fleshmonger, to support his reforms. The foundation of the 'Wiccamical' Prebends (which still exist) shows his affection for and personal links with Winchester College and New College, Oxford, the foundations of which he himself was a member. It can justly be claimed that he was a second founder of the cathedral itself: his episcopate was as vigorous as it was reforming. He left a considerable mark on the building – the screen behind the high altar (now adorned by the Piper tapestry), the panels in the north transept depicting bishops of Chichester (they all seem to be Sherburne), and the panels in the south transept, both by Lambert Barnard. The latter panels are medallion heads of the kings of England from William the Conqueror, and two scenes depicting the granting by Caedwalla of the see of Selsey to St Wilfrid and the confirmation by Henry VIII of the bishopric to Sherburne (a tactful gesture!). In the Lady Chapel there exists in the second

vault more work by Lambert Barnard, painting in foliage design, part of what was a larger scheme.

It includes the motto 'Manners makyth man', an indication of Sherburne's Wykehamist origins. Altogether, he was an enlightened bishop, anxious that the clergy should be learned as well as devout.

The effigy of Sherburne shows him in episcopal apparel (the arms include the pelican, which appears elsewhere in the cathedral, including the brass lectern). At his feet are 'bedesmen', praying for his soul.

ABOVE: *A painting by Lambert Barnard showing the kings of England from William the Conqueror with, above, two scenes from the cathedral's history. One of them, enlarged right, shows Henry VIII confirming Sherburne as Bishop of Chichester (a tactful gesture as Sherburne had employed Barnard!).* 8

LEFT: *The effigy of Bishop Sherburne from his monument in the south quire aisle.* 10

In the years following the Reformation, the task of maintaining the cathedral fabric was a constant difficulty. During the Civil War much damage was inflicted, especially to the interior, and the library was despoiled. There are signs still of Puritan depredation, and we know its extent from the evidence provided by Bruno Ryves, dean at the time. Later in the 17th century Christopher Wren took down and rebuilt the spire. The north-west tower was already in ruins, but Wren's plans for the west end were never realised, and the tower was eventually restored to a design by J.L. Pearson (died 1897) and completed by his son in 1901.

Considerable restoration was carried out in the 19th century, chiefly by R.C. Carpenter (who also built St Peter's Church to the north-west of the cathedral) and Joseph Butler. The building had its wooden galleries removed, and, after the fall of the spire in 1861, the reconstruction was carried out by Sir George Gilbert Scott.

Dean George Chandler (1830–59), who is commemorated by wrought ironwork in the quire, was responsible for the west window (1848). His successor, Dean Walter Farquhar Hook (1859–75), also contributed to the reordering of the interior, including the restoration of the Lady Chapel, to make the cathedral a more convenient and fitting place of worship. Hook's successors brought back the other chapels into use.

ABOVE: *John the Baptist, the central detail of the south transept window.* ⑨

LEFT: *The work of restoring the cathedral inside and out goes on day by day.*

It was Hook who vigorously promoted the repair and rebuilding of the tower and spire after the collapse of 1861. (The stalls were restored under the supervision of G.F. Bodley.) Sir George Gilbert Scott designed Hook's memorial marble catafalque chest in the south quire aisle, and the hour bell of the cathedral chimes, 'Great Walter', is named after Dean Hook. Weaknesses inherent in the original building were the fundamental cause of the 1861 disaster, and over the years much more of the stonework has decayed. After the Second World War extensive restoration work had to be undertaken, and there was an impressive response to an appeal for financial help.

Repairs and restoration, however, proved to be a lengthy and increasingly expensive task, so in 1965 the Cathedral Works Organisation was founded.

ABOVE: *The pulpit (1966) was designed by Geoffrey Clarke and Robert Potter.*

LEFT: *The scene in the nave after the spire had collapsed in 1861.*

BELOW: *The scene on 28 June 1866 as the old weathercock is hoisted to top out the rebuilt spire. The architect was Sir George Gilbert Scott (1811–78).*

The cathedral from the south showing St Richard's Walk.

The Treasury occupies what was once the Chapel of the Four Virgins on the east side of the north transept. The Worshipful Company of Goldsmiths gave generous financial assistance to enable the cathedral to house and display securely its own treasures as well as plate from churches in the diocese. Among the former are medieval chalices, patens, crozier heads and rings discovered in bishops' tombs during repair work in 1829–30; the latter include a pre-Reformation paten *c.*1500, from Donnington.

The room above the Treasury has been the cathedral library since 1951. In 1969 the Pilgrim Trust contributed substantially to its refurbishing. Latin books from the 16th and early 17th centuries, originally numbering about 900, form the core of the present collection. They were bequeathed in 1671 by John King to re-establish the library after the

*ABOVE: **Items from the Treasury.*** ⑰

*BELOW: **A 16th-century Spanish Dominican antiphoner, a book of chants and responses.*** ⑨

Civil War. John was the son of Bishop Henry King (1642–69), himself the friend and executor of the poet John Donne who left books from his own library to King. Other treasured volumes include a book which belonged to Archbishop Cranmer, and the large 16th-century antiphoner now displayed in the south transept.

Three famous musicians have been associated with Chichester: Thomas Weelkes, the distinguished Elizabethan composer (organist 1602–23), whose memorial is in the north transept, Thomas Kelway (organist 1720–44), buried in St Clement's Chapel, and Gustav Holst (1874–1934) who had close connections with Chichester, whose ashes are buried in the north transept. The offering of music by skilled singers is central to worship in Chichester Cathedral.

*LEFT: **The organ, showing the painted Renatus Harris pipes of 1678. It was restored in 1986 after a silence of 13 years.*** ⑦

In the later 20th century, successive deans worked to bring fine examples of modern painting and craftsmanship to the cathedral. These stand side by side with the magnificent art and architecture from centuries gone by.

One of the first modern additions is *The Baptism of Christ* (1951) by Hans Feibusch, on the south wall of the baptistry. The font was made by John Skelton in 1983. On the south wall of the baptistry is John Flaxman's memorial to the poet William Collins, who died in 1769. The altar frontal in St Clement's Chapel, *The Icon of Divine Light* (1973), is by Cecil Collins. It illustrates the painter's use of the concept of light, the icon and the sun's rays signifying God's gift of life to mankind. Michael Clark's conceptual series, *The Wounds of Christ*, was placed in different parts of the Cathedral in 1994.

The sole evidence of Renaissance work in the cathedral is a niche of *c.*1535, with tiny figures and arabesques, in the south nave aisle. On the wall near

St Richard's Porch is the Bradbridge brass of 1592. The tomb of John Arundel (Bishop 1459–78), from which the brass has disappeared, is in the sixth bay. Two sculpted stone panels of *c.*1125 in the south quire aisle represent the raising of Lazarus and Christ arriving at Bethany being greeted by Mary and Martha. The panels were perhaps part of a screen, and are the most distinguished monuments in the cathedral, very well preserved, lacking only the original colour on the garments and the jewels in the eyes. Displayed below the floor nearby is a fragment of a Roman mosaic of the 2nd century – a reminder of the Roman city of Noviomagus.

At the south end of the retroquire platform is the tomb of George Day (Bishop 1543–51; 1553–56), and at the north end, the tomb of Bishop William Barlow, who consecrated Archbishop Matthew Parker in 1559.

ABOVE: *The Chapel of St John the Baptist. The reredos (1984) is by Patrick Procktor and shows the baptism of Jesus.* ⑮

LEFT: *The font (1983), designed by John Skelton. The painting behind is* The Baptism of Christ *(1951) by Hans Feibusch.* ①

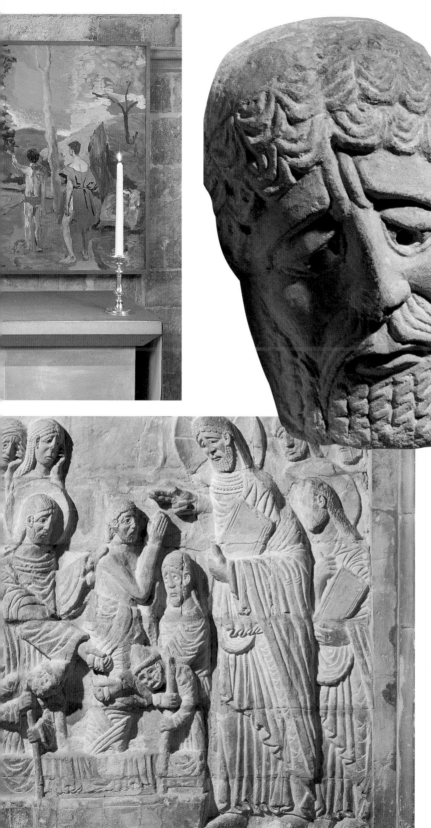

ABOVE:
The head of
Christ from a
Romanesque
carved panel
(c.1125),
depicting the
raising of
Lazarus. ⑩

LEFT:
The Lazarus
panel is one of
two fine 12th-
century carvings
in the south
quire aisle. ⑩

In the Chapel of St Mary Magdalene, the altar is by Robert Potter and the ornaments by Geoffrey Clarke. Above is Graham Sutherland's painting *Noli me Tangere* ('Touch me not'). Above the entrance to the Lady Chapel is the sculpture *Christ in Judgement* by Philip Jackson (1998). What is regarded as the tomb of Bishop Luffa is within the Lady Chapel. Above it is the memorial to Thomas Bickley (Bishop 1585–96). The sanctuary floor retains a few encaustic 13th-century tiles. The roof bosses in the two west bays are the earliest in the cathedral.

The retroquire is the site of the shrine of St Richard of Chichester (Bishop 1245–53) and also the burial place of Bishop George Bell. In the striking tapestry designed by Ursula Benker-Schirmer and woven at West Dean, Sussex, and Marktredwitz, Bavaria, in 1985, there are four main symbols: the chalice (St Richard); the candle (the light of the world); the fig tree (life and fruitfulness); the fish (Christ). The cross is in the centre, surrounded by a circle representing the cycle of life, itself completion and wholeness, but broken up at the top to open the way to eternity. The tapestry represents Anglo-German reconciliation and friendship, in memory of Bishop Bell's work for German refugees and his links with the German churches.

LEFT: *The retroquire, site of St Richard's shrine. The altar (1984), designed by Robert Potter, is of Purbeck marble.* ⑫

BELOW: *The sculpture* Christ in Judgement *(1998) by Philip Jackson.* ⑫

LEFT: *The Chapel of St Mary Magdalene houses Graham Sutherland's painting* Noli me Tangere *(Christ appearing to St Mary Magdalene after the Resurrection).*

In the north quire aisle is the memorial to William Otter, in whose brief but energetic episcopate (1836–40) the Theological College was founded. His main surviving monument is Bishop Otter College, now University College, Chichester. See also the Jacobean monument to John Cawley (died 1621), whose son (also commemorated) was among those who signed the death warrant of Charles I.

The high altar is by Robert Potter, and above it is the famous tapestry by John Piper. He suggested that the screen with its crest of medieval canopies would be an ideal setting for seven strips of tapestry which would not only introduce colour at the east end of the quire, but would also provide an appropriate symbolism. The subject is the Trinity (three central panels) represented by an equilateral triangle among flames, and related to this, symbols for the Father (a white light), the Son (a Tau Cross) and the Holy Spirit (a flame-like wing). In the flanking panels are symbols for the elements and the Evangelists. The tapestry was woven by Pinton Frères at Felletin, near Aubusson (Creuse), and was installed in 1966.

In the north nave aisle, the tomb of Joan, daughter of Robert de Vere, Earl of Oxford, dates from the late 13th century. It is one of

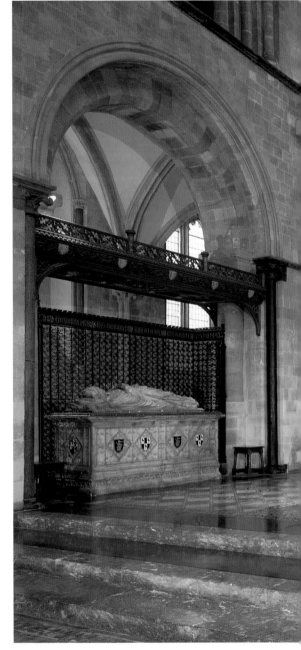

LEFT: In the north aisle stands a monument to William Huskisson, MP for Chichester who was killed by a train in 1830 at the opening of the Manchester and Liverpool Railway. ㉓

the earliest examples in England of a monument with 'weepers' on the sides of the tomb chest. At the west end of the aisle is the large statue by J.E. Carew of William Huskisson, shown in Roman dress. He was MP for Chichester, and was killed at the opening of the Manchester and Liverpool Railway in 1830 – the first person to be killed by a train.

St Michael's Chapel was re-dedicated in 1956 as the Sailors' Chapel, commemorating Sussex men who lost their lives at sea in the Second World War.

ABOVE: *The high altar by Robert Potter, and behind it the John Piper tapestry (1966) depicting the Holy Trinity.* ⑪

RIGHT: *The Arundel tomb. The 14th-century figures are probably Richard Fitzalan (died 1376) and his countess. Their joined hands inspired Philip Larkin's poem,* An Arundel Tomb. ㉒

RIGHT: *The window designed by Marc Chagall in 1978 illustrating Psalm 150.* ⑯

Nearly all the original glass has been lost. The west window (1847–8) is by William Wailes, and at the eastern end above the retroquire and in the Chapel of St Mary Magdalene are windows (1893–4) by C.E. Kempe, to whom there is a memorial under the Stratford screen in the south transept. The glass in Bishop Langton's south transept window was inserted in 1877, and came from Lorraine. Its colours are bright but the figures pallid.

The stained glass in the north nave aisle commemorates some significant figures in the history of the cathedral and diocese. They are by Christopher Webb, as is the window in St John's Chapel. In the Lady Chapel there is a complete set of Victorian windows designed and made by Clayton & Bell (1873–88). In the lower central panel of a window in the south quire aisle are the

arms of Edward More, Archdeacon of Lewes in 1528–31, the only ancient surviving glass in the cathedral.

The window on the north of the retro-quire was designed by Marc Chagall (1978) and executed by Charles of Marq at Reims. The window illustrates Psalm 150, 'O praise God in his holiness . . . Let everything that hath breath praise the Lord.' The dominant colour, red, suggests the glory which the whole creation, animate and inanimate, offers to God. David, the writer of psalms, rides on a donkey. The instruments mentioned in the psalm are to be seen in the window and the posture and character of the figures are typical of Chagall's work.

ABOVE: *The Flight into Egypt, part of a series of windows by Clayton & Bell in the Lady Chapel depicting scenes in the life of the Virgin.* ⑭

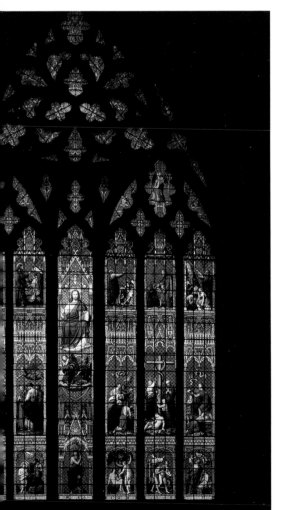

LEFT: *The south transept window depicting scenes from the Bible, from Adam and Eve to the Resurrection, was designed by C. Parrish and made in Metz in 1877.* ⑨

On leaving the west end of the cathedral, one passes the early 13th-century chapel of the Bishop's Palace. On the external wall of the south transept within the cloisters is a corbel table, renovated in 1932. The heads of George V, Lloyd George, Ramsay MacDonald and Stanley Baldwin are recognizable.

On the south wall of the cloisters are important monuments including one with the arms of King Henry VII (The House of the Royal Chantry priests). A further memorial to Bishop George Bell was the opening by his friend Pastor Niemöller, in 1977, of the Bishop Bell Rooms, which serve as the cathedral refectory.

East of the cloisters, bordering South Street, is the Vicars' Hall, the early 15th-century hall of the Vicars Choral. The main hall is now used for

ABOVE: *St Richard's Walk looking from the Cloisters towards Canon Lane. The first house has a medieval core; the second, the Organist's house, has a Georgian façade.*

LEFT: *All that remains of the 15th-century Vicars' Close is this attractive row of four cottages.*

TOP RIGHT: *The gardens of the Bishop Bell Rooms: the Cathedral refectory.* ㉖

RIGHT: *Canon Gate House at the entrance to the close from South Street.*

ABOVE: Dean John Treadgold represented in a modern gargoyle on the south wall of the nave.

a variety of cathedral functions, and the late 12th-century undercroft is now a restaurant. The entrance to the close from South Street is through an arch under Canon Gate House, a 15th-century building largely reconstructed in 1894 by Ewan Christian.

Vicars' Close nearby is also 15th century, but in 1825 its eastern range was given a new frontage on South Street and a wall erected in its place. By 1831 the rest of Vicars' Close, other than the present houses, was demolished.

On the left of Canon Lane, and set back from it, is the Chantry which is 13th-century in origin, and further along is the 15th-century Residentiary. The Deanery was built in 1725. At the end of Canon Lane is a gateway of 1327 leading into the Bishop's Palace. The early 19th-century house known as the Treasury was refurbished in 1999 as a children's education centre. The cathedral gift shop is in the base of the bell tower.

WHY A CATHEDRAL?

433
428
296
276
391